AMAZON RIVER WOLVES

NORTHWATER

CONSTANTINE ISSIGHOS

Copyright 2012 © Constantine Issighos. Published in Canada. Printed in U.S.A. No part of this book may be reproduced or transmitted in any form or by any means, electronic or mechanical, including photocopying, recording, and/or by any information storage and retrieval system except by a reviewer who may quote brief passages in a review to be printed in a magazine, newspaper, or on the web without written permission in writing from the author/publisher. For information, please contact www.awaqkunabooks.com

NorthWater is an imprint of Awaqkuna Books Inc.

Vol. 8 of THE AMAZON EXPLORATION SERIES:
AMAZON RIVER WOLVES

Library and Archives Canada

ISBN 978-0-9878599-7-6

Library and Archives Canada Cataloguing in Publication

ATTENTION CHILDRENS ASSOCIATIONS, BOOK STORES, PUBLIC OR PRIVATE LIBRARIES: quantity discounts are available on bulk purchases of this book series.

THE AMAZON EXPLORATION SERIES

Children's Books
by
Constantine Issighos

1. Upper Amazon Voyage by River Boat
2. The People of the River
3. The Children of the River
4. Amazon's Nature of Things
5. Echoes of Nature: a Beautiful Wild Habitat
6. The Amazon Rainforest
7. Amazonian Sisterhood
8. Amazon River Wolves
9. Amazonian Landscapes and Sunsets
10. Amazonian Canopy: the Roof of the World's Rainforest
11. Amazonian Tribes: a World of Difference
12. Birds and Butterflies of the Amazon
13. The Great Wonders of the Amazon
14. The Jaguar People
15. The Fresh Water Giants
16. The Call of the Shaman
17. Indigenous Families: Life in Harmony with Nature
18. Amazon in Peril
19. Giant Tarantulas and Centipedes
20. The Amazon Ethno-Botanical Garden
21. The Real Amazon Tribal Warriors

The Amazon River is regarded as *The River Sea;* it has a greater total flow of water than the next six largest rivers combined. It is the second longest river on Earth, the Nile River being the longest. The Amazon River and its tributaries support a diverse range of wildlife. The largest species of the river dwellers are the Giant Otter, the Pink Dolphin, the Black Caiman, and the Anaconda snake, which is found in its shallow waters. It is also home to the Arapaima and the notorious Piranha. Some of the fish such as the Arapaima already existed in the Jurassic Period. Today, they are found in the Upper Amazon and parts of Africa and Asia.

Giant Otters

Giant otters live in the rivers and tributaries of the Amazon rainforest of Brazil, Bolivia, Colombia, Ecuador, Guyana, and parts of Argentina, Paraguay, Peru, Suriname and Venezuela.

South American giant river otters are the largest and among the rarest and most endangered species. Male giant otters grow to a length of 2 meters (more than 6 feet) from head to tail, with females being a bit smaller. Fully grown otters can weigh more than 27 kilos (70 lbs).

The coat of the giant otters varies from reddish-brown to dark-brown to coffee colour. The fur is very dense which permits little or no water to reach the skin. Most otters are hunted for their fur pelts which are short and compact.

The large head of the giant otter has more of a domed skull than that of other otter species. The neck is strong and thick and the profile of the skull resembles that of a dog, thus its nickname Perro de Agua (water dog). Its nose is covered in fur with whiskers that help it to detect prey moving underwater. Both nostrils and ears can shut off when the otter is underwater.

Fully grown giant otters are not generally preyed upon by other carnivorous animals, though jaguars, large caimans and anacondas prey upon otter pups. The more dangerous predator is the human hunter, who hunts giant otters for their pelts.

Arapaima Giant Fish

Arapaima giant fish is also known as Paiche, and it is one of the largest freshwater fish in the world. This fish can be found wild in parts of Africa, Thailand and in the Amazon River basin of South America. It is a prehistoric species that first appeared in the Miocene Epoch 23 million years ago. It belongs to a much older family, the Osteoglossidas, which means that the Arapaima existed in the Jurassic Period. Therefore, its origins can be traced back to the Age of the Dinosaurs.

Arapaima can reach a length of more than 2 meters (15 feet) and weigh more than 200 kilos (450 lbs). Its scales are olive-green in colour and turn increasingly reddish towards the tail. This tail portion can grow up to 7 meters (21 feet) long on the largest specimens. More than half the weight of the fish is made up of boneless flesh, thus making it a popular food.

The Arapaima is a predatory fish that eats other fish, birds and animals such as monkeys. It hunts close to the surface since it needs to breathe oxygen from the air every 10 to 20 minutes. This does not prevent the Arapaima from frequently diving in search of food.

In the Upper Amazon of Peru, giant Arapaima fish can be found in the waters of the Pacaya-Samiria Reserve, where fishing for it is prohibited. This reserve is filled with an incredible diversity of animals, exotic birds; pink river dolphins, monkeys and a variety of fish species share their home with the Arapaima.

Pirahnas

The Piranhas (or Red Bellied Pirahnas) are a group of omnivorous freshwater fish living in parts of the Amazon River and its tributaries. They are best known not for their size but for their ferocity. They have short powerful jaws with razor sharp teeth.

As their name suggests they have a reddish line on their bellies. Traditionally, only 4 species—the Pristobrycon, Pyrocentrus, Pygopristis and the Serrasalmus—were considered to be true piranhas, due to their specialized teeth.

The total number of piranha species is not known, and new species continue to be discovered. However, half of the currently classified 60 nominal species of piranha remain questionable.

Some species of piranha have extremely broad geographic ranges, occurring in more than one major river basin, whereas others appear to have much more limited distributions.

Ecologically, piranhas are important components of the Amazonian River and its tributaries. Although largely restricted to lowland drainages, piranhas are widespread and inhabit diverse habitats within both deep and shallow water levels. Some piranha species are abundant locally and multiple species often occur together. As both predators and scavengers, piranhas influence their local lotic and lentic environments. There are many piranha species that are vegetarian, eating nuts that fall in the water by using their teeth to crack the shell. Although certain piranha species consume large quantities of nuts, since they thoroughly masticate and destroy all the seeds, they are not regarded as dispersers.

The piranha is usually portrayed as a vicious species of fish that hunts in large schools. This is actually used as a defence mechanism against the piranha's natural predators, such as the pink dolphin, the black caiman and giant Arapaima fish.

The Anaconda

In the Amazon rainforest, this giant snake is also known as Yucu-mama (Eunucles murimus) and it is the biggest and most well-known boa on the South American continent. The adult Anaconda can reach ten meters in length and weigh up to 250 kilos (550 lbs). If the Anaconda is not the longest snake species, it is definitely the heaviest. This great bulk is put to use for catching and for subduing a prey. They are constrictors, and they lie submerged along the shallow riverbanks to ambush their next meal. Constrictors do not crush their prey—jagged broken bones would damage their digestive systems.

In spite of its amazing appearance, the Anacondas it is not a poisonous snake. Although is considered to be a harmless, there have been occasions where it has attacked humans when it has been molested.

The Anacondas feed on caiman, peccary, deer, large birds or any other animal that it can reach. When the prey comes within striking distance, an Anaconda lunges, bites, and holds the animal while it throws several coils of its body around it. Then the Anaconda constricts, tighten the coils when the prey inhales, quickly suffocating it. Prey is then swallowed whole.

Due to its inoffensive nature, the indigenous natives use Anacondas to control rodents (like scare-crows). There are many legends and superstitions shared by the indigenous people about the Anaconda including two-headed, crown-wearing specimens.

Pink and Grey Dolphins

Of the five freshwater species of dolphins in the world, the pink and grey Amazon River dolphins are considered to be the most intelligent. These friendly, sensitive mammals with a brain capacity 40% larger than that of humans have lived in harmony with the people of the Amazon River and its tributaries for millennia.

One of the most endangered species in the Upper Peruvian Rainforest, the pink dolphin is strictly protected by Peruvian Forest Police, thus maintaining the survival of the Pink and Grey dolphins in their natural environment.

Ecological factors strongly influence social behaviour. Since the pink dolphin does not have any known natural predators—other than humans—they do not need to live in large groups. They engage in solitary hunting and feeding strategies during the high water season when their prey fish disperse into the floodplains. At times, they are found in small groups of 5 to 8 animals, as I have witnessed on the

Maranon River between Yurimaguas and Iquitos. They are often seen cooperatively hunting with grey dolphins.

Grey dolphins are gregarious animals and exhibit strong ties with their own kind. They seem to practice a polyandrous breeding system and females tend to be a bit larger than males. They appear to have a matriarchic order.

Both the Pink and Grey dolphins figure prominently in the local mythologies and their reputation varies from one tributary to another. There are local legends regarding pink dolphins pushing people to shore after their canoes have capsized. In some floodlands, the pink dolphins are considered as unpredictable brujos or wizards. In other locations they are seen as benign and helpful semi-divine beings. The dolphins are regarded as "sacred" animals by various indigenous tribes.

Black Caiman

This fresh water giant is the larger predator in the Amazon river system. It has no enemies other than man. It can attack and eat piranha, capybara, giant otters and humans. It can grow up to 7 meters (20feet) and can reach (I ton) 2.200 lbs in weight.

Throughout the Amazon region there are scattered pockets of black caiman, but because of human hunting, fully grown adults are rare. In the last 75 years the trading of caiman skin has brought their numbers to dangerously low levels.

The majority of females build mound nests of soil or sand, but some individual caiman excavate holes to use as nests. The size of the nest mound increases as the female black caiman increases in size—females usually lay about 40 eggs at a time. The consequences of hunting adult black caiman go beyond the killing of the animal itself. When the adult animal is killed, its nest with eggs is ravaged by predators in the absence of the protection of the mother caiman.

Black caiman are endangered throughout the Amazon region. For centuries they have been hunted for their leathery hides to make shoes and boots, wallets and belts. As in the case of snakes, caimans are often misunderstood and have been killed by fearful humans.

The Jaguar

The jaguar lives in the dense understory layer of the Amazon rainforest, in rivers and in swamps. Its diet is grown mammals, fish, frogs, turtles and small gators. The jaguar has hooked claws for climbing and catching fish.

Jaguars spend a lot of time swimming. They are a water-loving cat where they catch a considerable portion of their prey, like caiman and fish, for their daily consumption.

The Amazon Exploration Series *Constantine Issighos*

AMAZONIAN GIANT OTTER

Constantine Issighos *The Amazon Exploration Series*

The Amazon Exploration Series *Constantine Issighos*

Amazon River Wolves 17

Constantine Issighos   *The Amazon Exploration Series*

AMAZONIAN PIRAÑA

The Amazon Exploration Series   *Constantine Issighos*

Amazon River Wolves   *31*

The Amazon Exploration Series   *Constantine Issighos*

Amazon River Wolves

The Amazon Exploration Series   *Constantine Issighos*

Amazon River Wolves   43

www.ingramcontent.com/pod-product-compliance
Lightning Source LLC
Chambersburg PA
CBHW041754040426
42446CB00001B/28